New Testament

Dedication

For my wife and family and your
undying faith . . .
Without you this book would
be nonexistant.

СР

Copyright © 1996 by Educational Publishing Concepts, Inc.,
Wheaton, Illinois

Published in Wheaton, Illinois by Victor Books/SP Publications, Inc., Wheaton Illinois

ISBN 1-56476-555-5

Printed in the United States of America

1 2 3 4 5 6 7 — 00 99 98 97 96

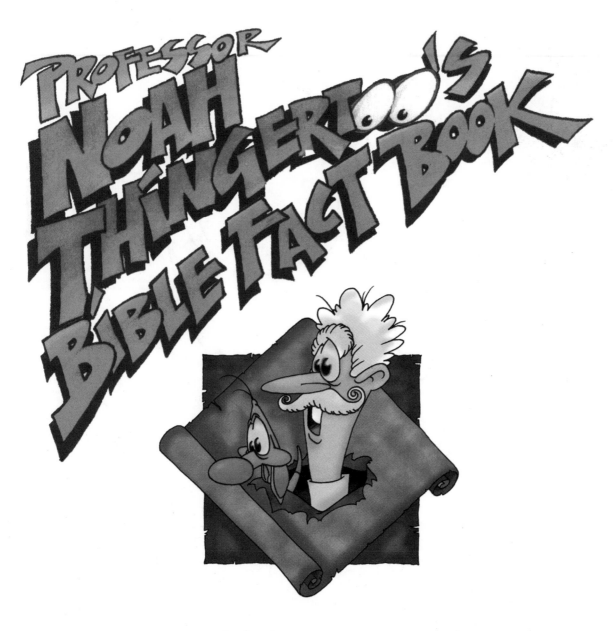

Professor Noah Thingertoo's Bible Fact Book

New Testament

Written and Illustrated by
Christopher Gray

VICTOR BOOKS

A DIVISION OF SCRIPTURE PRESS PUBLICATIONS INC.
USA CANADA ENGLAND

BABY JESUS

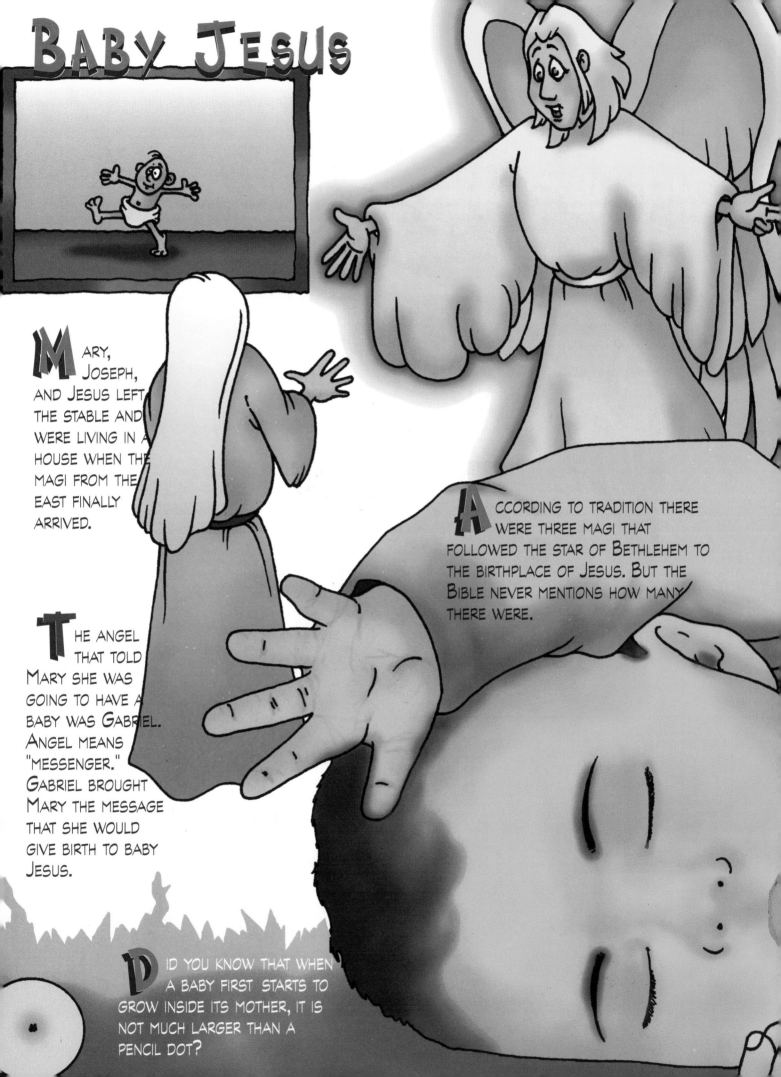

MARY, JOSEPH, AND JESUS LEFT THE STABLE AND WERE LIVING IN A HOUSE WHEN THE MAGI FROM THE EAST FINALLY ARRIVED.

THE ANGEL THAT TOLD MARY SHE WAS GOING TO HAVE A BABY WAS GABRIEL. ANGEL MEANS "MESSENGER." GABRIEL BROUGHT MARY THE MESSAGE THAT SHE WOULD GIVE BIRTH TO BABY JESUS.

ACCORDING TO TRADITION THERE WERE THREE MAGI THAT FOLLOWED THE STAR OF BETHLEHEM TO THE BIRTHPLACE OF JESUS. BUT THE BIBLE NEVER MENTIONS HOW MANY THERE WERE.

DID YOU KNOW THAT WHEN A BABY FIRST STARTS TO GROW INSIDE ITS MOTHER, IT IS NOT MUCH LARGER THAN A PENCIL DOT?

GOD'S SON, JESUS WAS BORN IN A STABLE IN BETHLEHEM.

JOSEPH WAS A CARPENTER, AND WHEN JESUS WAS OLD ENOUGH, HE WOULD HAVE PASSED ON THE TRADE TO HIM.

JESUS' FIRST BED WAS AN ANIMAL FEED TROUGH.

GIFTS OF GOLD, FRANKINCENSE AND MYRRH WERE GIFTS WORTHY OF A KING! JOSEPH PROBABLY USED THE GIFTS TO SUPPORT HIS SMALL FAMILY IN EGYPT UNTIL THE DEATH OF HEROD.

WHEN A WOMAN IS PREGNANT THE AMOUNT OF BLOOD IN HER BODY INCREASES BY 25%. THAT IS BECAUSE OF THE GROWING BABY AND ITS DEVELOPMENT!

HOBBY CORNER

PRAYER IN A BOTTLE!

YOU'VE HEARD OF A MESSAGE IN A BOTTLE? WELL, HOW ABOUT A PRAYER IN A BOTTLE?

ONE A PIECE OF PAPER WRITE DOWN YOUR FAVORITE PRAYER. INCLUDE YOUR NAME, ADDRESS AND DATE AND ROLL IT UP. STICK THE ROLLED UP PRAYER PAPER INTO AN UNUSED BOTTLE, PUT A CORK IN THE TOP AND DROP IT INTO THE RIVER OR THE SEA. JUST THINK OF IT! ANYONE, ANYWHERE IN THE WORLD, MIGHT EVENTUALLY FIND YOUR PRAYER IN A BOTTLE AND IT COULD EVEN CHANGE THEIR LIFE!

JESUS TEACHES IN THE TEMPLE

JOSEPH WAS RESPONSIBLE FOR THE EDUCATION OF JESUS AS A CHILD.

JOSEPH WAS PROBABLY NOT ONLY JESUS' TEACHER IN THE WAYS OF A CARPENTER, BUT ALSO HIS PRINCIPLE TEACHER IN THE WAYS OF GOD'S COVENANT WITH ISRAEL.

DID YOU KNOW THAT THE 39 BOOKS OF THE OLD TESTAMENT WERE THE VERY BOOKS FROM WHICH JESUS HIMSELF READ?

RABBI MEANS "TEACHER" OR "MASTER" WHICH WAS A TITLE OF RESPECT AMONG THE JEWS. JESUS' TEACHING WAS SO DYNAMIC THAT MANY REFERRED TO HIM WITH THIS HONORABLE TITLE.

DID YOU KNOW THAT THE TERM "SCAPEGOAT" COMES FROM A RELIGIOUS CELEBRATION THAT THE JEWS USED TO OBSERVE IN THE DAYS OF HEROD'S TEMPLE? THEY USED TO SEND A GOAT THAT SYMBOLICALLY CARRIED THE SINS OF THE JEWISH PEOPLE OUT INTO THE DESERT WHERE IT WOULD ESCAPE WITH ALL THEIR SINS.

When Jesus was just a little boy He knew more about God than the teachers in the temple.

Excavations in Israel have unearthed terra cotta toys. Terra cotta is a hard, semifired, ceramic clay that is brownish orange in color, and may have been used in toys that Jesus played with.

A ram's horn, or shophar, is blown like a horn at the start of every Jewish religious festival.

A rabbi, or teacher, studies a book called the Torah. The word "Torah" means teaching. The Torah consists of five books of the Bible Genesis, Exodus, Leviticus, Numbers, and Deuteronomy. Christians call this the "Pentateuch" which is a Greek word that simply means "five books."

HOBBY CORNER

MAKE YOUR OWN TERRA COTTA TOYS!

You'll need:
※ Mexican Pottery Clay (You can get this at your local craft store for about $8.00)
¥ Sunshine

Break off a chunk of clay and knead it in your hands. Form it into the shape of an animal or toy that you'd like to play with. Set the finished toy out in the sunshine to dry.

TIP: The bigger the chunk of clay, and the heavier and thicker the toy is, the longer it will take to dry. When it's completely dry and you're ready to play, remember, this was one of the only toys that the children of Israel had to play with.

THE TEMPLE IN THE TIME OF JESUS

THE SABBATH IS SATURDAY, THE SEVENTH DAY OF THE WEEK TO THE JEWS AND OBSERVED AS A DAY OF REST AND WORSHIP. TO MOST CHRISTIANS THE SABBATH DAY IS THE FIRST DAY OF THE WEEK, SUNDAY.

THE SADDUCEES DID NOT BELIEVE IN THE RESURRECTION OF THE DEAD SINCE IT WAS NOT MENTIONED IN THE LAW OF MOSES. THEY DID NOT BELIEVE IN REWARDS OR PUNISHMENTS AFTER DEATH. THEY DIDN'T EVEN BELIEVE IN SPIRITS OR ANGELS. THIS IS WHAT CAUSED THE CONFLICT BETWEEN THEM AND THE PHARISEES. THE SADDUCEES WENT BY THE BOOK AND TO THE LETTER. THE PHARISEES, HOWEVER, CONSIDERED TRADITIONS ALMOST AS IMPORTANT AS THE LAW ITSELF.

JESUS AND THE PHARISEES OFTEN BUMPED HEADS WHEN IT CAME TO THE MOSAIC LAW, BUT NEVER DID JESUS SEPARATE HIMSELF FROM IT. UNLIKE THE PHARISEES, JESUS EMPHASIZED GOD'S LOVE THOUGH HE DID WARN OF GOD'S JUDGMENT. (MATTHEW 7:21)

THE BIGGEST AND GRANDEST TEMPLE WAS BUILT BY KING HEROD THE GREAT IN ABOUT 9 B.C. IT WAS THE VERY SAME TEMPLE IN WHICH MARY AND JOSEPH FOUND JESUS TALKING TO A GROUP OF WISE MEN AND TEACHERS WHEN HE WAS ONLY TWELVE YEARS OLD.

THE PHARISEES OF JESUS' TIME WERE VERY STRICT TEACHERS OF THE LAW. THEY ENFORCED, WITH EXTREMITY AND GREAT VIGOR, LAWS SUCH AS NOT WORKING ON THE SABBATH.

T HE SADDUCEES WERE A PRIESTLY JEWISH SECT IN THE SECOND CENTURY B.C. THAT PRACTICED ONLY THE MOSAIC LAW. THEY WERE A POWERFUL GROUP, AND MOST OF THEM WERE WEALTHY BEFORE THEY BECAME SADDUCEES.

T HE SADDUCEES ACCEPTED ROMAN RULE, WHICH IS WHERE THEY RECEIVED MOST OF THEIR POWER. THEY HAD A TEMPLE GUARD, AND IN ONE CASE THE SADDUCEES WERE RESPONSIBLE FOR THROWING TWO OF JESUS' DISCIPLES IN JAIL OVERNIGHT FOR HEALING A CRIPPLED MAN AND PREACHING WITHIN THE TEMPLE.

J ESUS WAS KNOWN TO DEFY THE LAWS OF THE PHARISEES. HE ONCE HEALED A MAN WHO HAD BEEN CRIPPLED AND INCAPABLE OF WALKING FOR 38 YEARS SAYING, "RISE, TAKE UP YOUR PALLET AND WALK." (JOHN 5:8)

D ID YOU KNOW   IT WAS DAVID'S SON, SOLOMON WHO ORDERED A TEMPLE TO BE BUILT IN THE SAME FASHION AS A PORTABLE TENT? THE TENT WAS CALLED A "TABERNACLE," AND THE PEOPLE OF ISRAEL USED TO HOUSE THE ARK OF THE COVENANT WITHIN IT BACK IN THE DAYS WHEN THE ISRAELITES TRAVELED THE LAND FREQUENTLY. THE TEMPLE WAS CALLED, OF COURSE, KING SOLOMON'S TEMPLE.

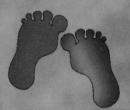

FOR SOME TIME PETER HAD SOLD LOCAL PLANTS WHICH SALTED FISH IN PREPARATION FOR EXPORT TO OTHER CITIES AS FAR AWAY AS ROME.

AT LEAST FOUR OF JESUS TWELVE DISCIPLES WERE FISHERMEN.

PETER WAS A PRACTICAL COMMERICAL FISHERMAN AND HE KNEW ALL THE SIGNS THAT TELL AN EXPERIENCED FISHERMAN THEIR TIME AND LABOR WOULD BE WASTED IF FISHING CONTINUED. JESUS, HOWEVER, SUGGESTED TO PETER THAT THE BOAT BE TAKEN BACK OUT AND THE NETS BE LOWERED FOR A CATCH.

DID YOU KNOW A CATFISH WILL EAT ANYTHING THAT SMELLS BAD? IT'S TRUE! A CATFISH'S PURPOSE IN NATURE IS TO CLEAN UP THE BOTTOM OF LAKES AND RIVERS. THEY ELIMINATE THE ROTTING CARCASSES THERE, AND IF THEY DIDN'T THE CARCASSES WOULD TAKE AWAY THE OXYGEN IN THE WATER AND ALL THE FISH WOULD DIE!

A BABY FISH IS CALLED 'FRY'.

HOBBY CORNER

"GONE FISHING"

WHAT YOU'LL NEED: PAPER, STRING, SCISSORS, PAPER CLIP, TAPE, STICK, AND CRAYONS.

CUT OUT A 6 INCH SQUARE OF PAPER AND MAKE A DOT IN THE CENTER. FOLD ALL CORNERS TO THE CENTER POINTS. OPEN TWO ADJOINING CORNERS AND CUT SLITS FROM THE CORNER TO THE FOLD LINE, NOW, AT THIS POINT YOU CAN MAKE TWO KINDS OF FISH. THE FIRST IS THE FINNED FISH AND FOR THIS ONE YOU'LL NEED TO FOLD THE TWO INNER WEDGES TOWARD THE CENTER, THE OUTSIDE WEDGES ARE THE FINS. THE SECOND IS THE TAILED FISH AND FOR THIS ONE YOU'LL NEED TO FOLD THE TWO OUTSIDE WEDGES TO THE CENTER SO THE OTHER TWO WEDGES BECOME THE TAIL. TAPE DOWN ALL THE FLAPS. COLOR SOME SCALES ON YOUR FISH. TIE A LENGTH OF STRING TO YOUR STICK AND TIE THE PAPER CLIP TO THE OTHER END OF THE STRING. NOW YOU HAVE A FISHING POLE TO CATCH THE FISH BY CLIPPING THE PAPER CLIP TO THE NOSE OF YOUR FISH.

MIRACLES OF JESUS

PETER'S MOTHER-IN-LAW GOT UP AND STARTED DOING CHORES AFTER JESUS HEALED HER OF A BAD FEVER.

HOW MANY LOAVES OF BREAD WERE USED TO FEED FIVE THOUSAND PEOPLE? NEXT TIME YOU SIT DOWN FOR DINNER THINK ABOUT THIS: YOUR DINNER PLATE IS A FAIRLY NEW INVENTION. BEFORE THE FIFTEENTH CENTURY, IT WAS CUSTOMARY TO EAT YOUR DINNER OFF OF A THICK SLICE OF STALE BREAD. THEY CALLED IT A "TRENCHER," AND IT WAS PROBABLY TASTY BECAUSE IT SOAKED UP THE JUICE.

WHEN THE DISCIPLES FIRST SAW JESUS WALKING ON WATER THEY THOUGHT HE WAS A GHOST.

THE MOST MENTIONED MIRACLE IN THE NEW TESTAMENT WAS THE RESURRECTION OF JESUS.

JESUS PERFORMED HIS VERY FIRST MIRACLE IN CANA.

JESUS SAID, "PEACE BE STILL!" AND CALMED A STORM . ON THE BEAUFORT SCALE, A SCALE RECOGNIZED INTERNATIONALLY FOR DESCRIBING WIND SPEEDS, A STORM CAN CAUSE WIDESPREAD DAMAGE, REACH SPEEDS UP TO 75 MILES PER HOUR, AND IS ONLY ONE CLASS BELOW A HURRICANE.

DID YOU KNOW THE AVERAGE MOTHER WALKS 10 MILES A DAY AROUND THE HOUSE AS SHE DOES HER CHORES? SHE ALSO WALKS 4 MILES AND SPENDS 25 HOURS A YEAR JUST MAKING BEDS.

GOD'S GLORY AND SALVATION, AND A MORE SCIENTIFIC DEFINITION OF A MIRACLE IS A NATURAL PHENOMENON THAT APPEARS TO DEFEAT NATURAL LAWS.

JESUS DID MANY MIRACLES TO SHOW PEOPLE GOD'S POWER AND LOVE.

I CAN SEE!

AFTER JESUS HEALED THE BLIND MAN OF BETHSAIDA, THE MAN SAID THAT PEOPLE LOOKED LIKE TREES WALKING.

HOBBY CORNER

TREE PEOPLE

WHAT YOU'LL NEED:
PAPER
A CANDLE STICK
GREEN WATER COLOR PAINT
A STRAW

THE BLIND MAN THAT JESUS GAVE THE GIFT OF SIGHT THOUGHT THAT PEOPLE LOOKED LIKE WALKING TREES, RIGHT? LET'S DO AN EXPERIMENT THAT WILL MAKE A STICK MAN FIGURE LOOK LIKE A TREE. FIRST TAKE A PIECE OF PAPER AND USING THE CANDLE STICK LIKE A PENCIL, DRAW A STICK MAN ON YOUR PAPER. YOU CAN'T REALLY SEE IT YET, CAN YOU? NEITHER COULD THE BLIND MAN. NOW DAB A GLOB OF THE GREEN PAINT RIGHT IN THE CENTER OF YOUR PAPER. NEXT TAKE YOUR STRAW AND BLOW THE PAINT INTO LITTLE BRANCH-LIKE STREAMS ALL OVER THE PAPER. NOW LOOK! THE PAINT DOES NOT ADHERE TO THE WAX, SO THE INVISIBLE STICK MAN CAN NOW BE SEEN! NOT A MIRACLE, BUT IT SURE WAS FUN, WASN'T IT?

FEASTS

PASSOVER REFERS TO THE INCIDENT IN GENESIS WHERE THE ANGEL OF DEATH PASSED OVER THE HOMES OF GOD'S PEOPLE, TAKING ONLY THE FIRSTBORN OF THE EGYPTIANS.

THE WORD PENTECOST IS A GREEK WORD MEANING FIFTIETH. THE PENTACOST IS THE CHRISTIAN FEAST CELEBRATED FIFTY DAYS AFTER EASTER AND TEN DAYS AFTER THE ASCENSION OF JESUS CHRIST TO HEAVEN.

THE LAST SUPPER THAT JESUS HAD WITH HIS 12 DICIPLES WAS A PASSOVER MEAL.

JESUS GREATLY ENJOYED A FEAST OR A PARTY, WHICH DREW SOME CRITICISM (MATT 11:19; LUKE 7:34).

DID YOU KNOW THAT EVEN THE GLUE ON ISRAELI POSTAGE STAMPS IS CERTIFIED KOSHER? (ACCORDING TO JEWISH LAW IT IS FIT FOR USE)

NEHEMIAH SAID THAT ALL FEAST DAYS ARE HOLY TO THE LORD YOUR GOD.

GRAPES HAVE BEEN DRIED INTO RAISINS AS FAR BACK AS THE BRONZE AGE. WHEN GRAPES WERE OUT OF SEASON RAISINS WERE THE CHOICE OF FRUIT BECAUSE THEY WERE EASILY PRESERVED.

GRAPE VINES WERE GROWN THROUGHOUT THE HOLY LANDS NOT ONLY AS FRUIT, BUT ALSO FOR WINEMAKING. IN FACT, PALESTINE WAS RENOWNED FOR ITS WINES.

THE JEWISH PEOPLE CELEBRATE GOD'S LOVE AND PROTECTION THROUGH SEVERAL FEASTS.

DID YOU KNOW THAT A GALLON OF WINE WEIGHS LESS IN THE SUMMER THAN IT DOES IN THE WINTER?

OLIVES WERE USED AS A DELICIOUS FRUIT TO EAT, AND THIER OIL WAS A PRECIOUS COMMODITY.

HOBBY CORNER

MAKE YOUR OWN SILVER GOBLET!

WHAT YOU WILL NEED:

A SMALL PIECE OF CORRUGATED CARDBOARD, PLASTIC FOAM CUP, A PENCIL, SAFETY SCISSORS, LARGE EMPTY THREAD SPOOL, GLUE, 18 INCH LENGTH OF ALUMINUM FOIL

FOR THE GOBLET'S BASE TRACE THE TOP OF YOUR FOAM CUP ON THE PIECE OF CARDBOARD, THEN CUT IT OUT. THE STEM OF YOUR GOBLET IS GOING TO BE MADE FROM THE THREAD SPOOL BY GLUING IT TO THE CENTER OF THE CARDBOARD BASE. THEN APPLY A GOOD AMOUNT OF GLUE TO THE BOTTOM OF THE FOAM CUP. PLACE IT OVER THE TOP OF THE THREAD SPOOL AND PRESS THE TWO TOGETHER FIRMLY. LET IT DRY AND COME BACK TO FINISH IN ABOUT A HALF HOUR. AFTER THE GLUE HAS DRIED, PLACE THE GOBLET AT THE CENTER OF YOUR ALUMINUM FOIL, WRAP IT AROUND THE BASE, AND CONTINUE WRAPPING UNTIL YOU HAVE COVERED THE ENTIRE GOBLET.

IF YOU WISH TO REALLY DRINK FROM YOUR SILVER GOBLET, JUST PLACE A CLEAR PLASTIC CUP INSIDE AND EVERY TIME YOU USE IT, REMEMBER THE IMPORTANCE OF FEASTS IN TIMES OF JESUS.

ACCORDING TO LUKE'S GOSPEL JESUS NOT ONLY HAD PRIVATE COUNCIL WITH PILATE AS HE GAVE HIS TESTIMONY, BUT HE WAS ALSO SENT TO KING HEROD ANTIPAS, WHO WAS THEN IN JERUSALEM FOR THE PASSOVER, AND INTERROGATED BY HIM.

IN THE GARDEN OF GETHSEMANE, JESUS PRAYED THAT IF GOD WERE WILLING HE MIGHT BE SPARED HIS AGONY.

THE SOLDIERS GAVE JESUS A SCARLET ROBE, A CROWN OF THORNS, AND A REED FOR A SCEPTER.

PILATE WAS CONVINCED THAT JESUS DID NOT DESERVE PUNISHMENT.

IT WAS A ROMAN SOLDIER THAT LOOKED UPON THE FACE OF JESUS AFTER HE DIED AND SAID, "TRULY THIS MAN WAS A SON OF GOD."

HOBBY CORNER

A SOAP SCULPTURE CROSS!

WHAT YOU WILL NEED:
(1) POWDERED LAUNDRY SOAP
(2) WATER

USING A GOOD SIZED MIXING BOWL, POUR IN TWO CUPS OF SOAP AND ADD A TEASPOON OF WATER. NOW USE YOUR HANDS TO MOLD THE SOAP INTO A BALL. ADD A LITTLE MORE WATER WITH THE TEASPOON AS NEEDED. WHEN YOU FEEL LIKE THE SOAP BALL IS READY FOR SCULPTING, SEPARATE IT INTO TWO PIECES, ONE SLIGHTLY BIGGER THAN THE OTHER. NOW ROLL ONE OF THE SOAP PIECES INTO A LONG CYLINDER SHAPE. THIS WILL BE THE CENTER PIECE OF THE CROSS. NEXT ROLL THE OTHER SOAP PIECE INTO A CYLINDER, PLACE IT OVER THE OTHER CYLINDER IN THE SHAPE OF A CROSS, AND MOLD THE TWO PIECES TOGETHER WITH YOUR FINGERTIPS. LET IT DRY OVERNIGHT, AND EACH TIME YOU LOOK AT, OR PICK UP THIS NEW CROSS OF YOURS, REMEMBER THAT JESUS DIED FOR YOU BECAUSE HE LOVES YOU!

THE COMING OF THE HOLY SPIRIT

DID YOU KNOW THAT ALL WHO ARE BAPTIZED RECEIVE "THE GIFT OF THE HOLY SPIRIT"?

JESUS TELLS HIS DISCIPLES TO "RECEIVE THE HOLY SPIRIT" AS HE IS LEAVING. THIS MEANS THAT INSTEAD OF THEM HAVING JESUS WITH THEM, THEY WILL HAVE THE HOLY SPIRIT.

THE DISCIPLES HEARD A SOUND LIKE WIND AND SAW TONGUES OF FIRE TOUCHING EACH OF THEM. AS THE SPIRIT FILLED THEM WITH POWER, THEY KNEW IT WAS THE WORK OF GOD.

SEVEN WEEKS AFTER THE CRUCIFIXION, ON THE DAY OF PENTECOST, THE DISCIPLES RECEIVED THE NEW POWER JESUS HAD TOLD THEM ABOUT THE COMING OF THE HOLY SPIRIT.

THAT SAME DAY ABOUT 3,000 PEOPLE WERE BAPTIZED BECAUSE OF WHAT THEY HAD SEEN AND HEARD.

The Holy Spirit took the form of a dove at Jesus' baptism. This bird has remained a symbol of the Holy Spirit.

Jesus sent the Holy Spirit to help Christians live for Him.

The dove symbolizes peace, love, and forgiveness.

HOBBY CORNER

CREATE YOUR OWN HOLY SPIRIT T-SHIRT

What you will need:

A t-shirt made from 50% synthetic fibers.
Transfer fabric-marking crayons (available at most fabric stores)
Typing paper
Cardborad that will fit inside the shirt.
An iron

Using the crayons, draw a picture of a dove on your typing papaer, be sure and press hard. Slide the cardboard into the shirt and lay your drawing face down on the front of the shirt.

With the hot iron transfer the drawing to the shirt by ironing smoothly over the paper several times. Let the drawing paper cool, then peel it away. Wear your new t-shirt proudly! You are a Christian and that's something to show off. You have the power of the Holy Spirit.

PERSECUTION OF THE EARLY CHURCH

THE FIRST CHRISTIANS WERE JEWISH PEOPLE. THEN THE APOSTLES STARTED PREACHING ABOUT JESUS TO PEOPLE WHO WEREN'T JEWS. THEY WERE CALLED GENTILES.

THE WORD APOSTLE MEANS "MESSENGER."

EARLY CHRISTIANS WERE TORTURED OR KILLED BECAUSE OF THEIR FAITH.

JESUS CHOSE 12 MEN TO BE HIS APOSTLES. HE GAVE THEM THE POWER TO HEAL AND TEACH IN HIS

THE JEWISH LEADERS DID NOT BELIEVE THAT JESUS WAS THE SON OF GOD AND THAT'S WHY THEY FOUGHT WITH THE CHRISTIANS.

A MAN NAMED STEPHEN WAS THE FIRST MARTYR. A MARTYR IS SOMEONE WHO IS KILLED BECAUSE OF WHAT HE BELIEVES IN. STEPHEN WAS STONED TO DEATH, A COMMON PUNISHMENT IN JESUS' TIME, BECAUSE HE BELIEVED IN JESUS AND CHRISTIANITY.

HOBBY CORNER

CAN YOU SEPARATE PEPPER FROM SALT WITH A SPOON?

IT WAS DIFFICULT TO BE A CHRISTIAN WHEN THE EARLY CHURCH WAS BEING PERSECUTED. TO SHOW YOU AN EXAMPLE OF HOW DIFFICULT IT WAS FOR THE EARLY CHRISTIANS WE'RE GOING TO TRY TO SEPARATE PEPPER FROM SALT USING A SPOON. SO, BEFORE YOU READ THE NEXT PARAGRAPH, GO AHEAD AND TRY IT. POUR OUT A SMALL PILE OF SALT, THEN ADD SOME PEPPER INTO THE PILE. MIX THEM TOGETHER. TRY TO SEPARATE THE PEPPER FROM THE SALT USING ONLY A SPOON.

IT WAS VERY DIFFICULT TO DO, WASN'T IT? IT WAS HARD FOR THE EARLY CHRISTIANS TO FIND A PLACE TO WORSHIP, BUT GOD HELPED THEM TO FIND WAYS TO KEEP FAITH AND TO ACCOMPLISH THINGS THAT SEEMED NEARLY IMPOSSIBLE.

NOW LET'S FINISH OUR EXPERIMENT. RUB YOUR SPOON AGAINST A SWEATER AND THEN HOLD IT OVER THE PILE OF SALT AND PEPPER. SEE WHAT HAPPENS? THE PEPPER SEPARATES FROM THE SALT WITH STATIC ELECTRICITY BECAUSE IT IS LIGHTER THAN THE SALT. THIS IS A GOOD EXAMPLE OF HOW THE EARLY CHRISTIANS SAW THE DIFFICULTIES OF WORSHIP, BUT MADE THINGS POSSIBLE BY THEIR FAITH IN GOD.

After they swam to shore Paul was gathering sticks for a fire when he was bitten by a deadly viper! He didn't die from the bite though. In fact, he didn't even have a mark where the snake had bitten him!

Did you know that scientists in China claim they can predict the weather with about 80% accuracy by monitoring the croaking of frogs?

A small hurricane releases the same amount of energy as the explosions of six atomic bombs per second!

HOBBY CORNER

MAKE A BOAT LIKE PAUL'S!

WHAT YOU WILL NEED:

A PIECE OF WHITE TYPING PAPER
A CRAYON (ANY COLOR)
SAFETY SCISSORS
A RULER

FIRST, USING YOUR RULER AND CRAYON, MEASURE A 5.75 INCH SQUARE AND COLOR IT IN. NEXT TAKE YOUR SCISSORS, CUT THE SQUARE INTO TWO SEPARATE TRIANGLES AND LAY ONE WHITE SIDE UP. NOW BRING THE OPPOSITE CORNERS TOGETHER CREATING A CREASE, BUT DON'T FORGET TO UNFOLD IT. THEN TAKE THE TOP POINT OF THE TRIANGLE AND FOLD IT DOWN TO WHERE THE CREASE MEETS THE BOTTOM EDGE. NOW FOLD THE LEFT TRIANGLE UP ALONG THE LEFT EDGE OF THE MIDDLE TRIANGLE, AND MAKE A CREASE. DO THE SAME WITH THE RIGHT SIDE, AND YOU SHOULD HAVE A DIAMOND SHAPE. NOW BRING THE BOTTOM POINT UP TO THE DIAMOND'S CENTER; CREASE IT, AND THEN UNFOLD IT TO FORM A BASE. NOW TURN IT AROUND, AND YOU HAVE JUST CREATED PAUL'S BOAT! PUT IT SOMEWHERE IN YOUR BEDROOM, AND EACH TIME YOU SEE IT, YOU'LL REMEMBER THE STORY OF PAUL'S SHIPWRECK.

THE MISSIONARY JOURNEY OF PAUL

PAUL'S FIRST JOURNEY WAS TO CYPRUS AND ANTIOCH. HE WAS SPREADING THE WORD OF JESUS AND HIS TEACHINGS.

IN THE 30 YEARS OF PAUL'S MISSIONARY WORK, HE FOUNDED CHURCHES IN 20 CITIES OF THE ROMAN EMPIRE!

HIS LAST JOURNEY WAS TO ROME TO STAND TRIL. WHILE HE WAS THERE, UNDER HOUSE ARREST, HE SPREAD THE WORD OF GOD AND TALKED ABOUT JESUS' TEACHINGS.

PAUL AND HIS FRIEND SILAS WERE ONCE ARRESTED AND PUT IN JAIL FOR DISTURBING THE PEACE. WHILE THEY WERE IN JAIL THEY WERE PRAYING WHEN ALL OF A SUDDEN THE PRISON WAS DESTROYED BY A GREAT EARTHQUAKE. PAUL AND SILAS WERE HARMED LITTLE, AND EVEN WENT HOME WITH THE JAILER TO HAVE SOME DINNER!

AFTER PAUL WAS SAVED, HE SPENT HIS LIFE TRAVELING THROUGHOUT THE WORLD PREACHING ABOUT GOD.

IF YOU WERE BORN WITH A HOOKED NOSE IN ANCIENT ROME, YOU WOULD HAVE BEEN CONSIDERED TO BE A LEADER.

IF THERE WERE ANY TREES CLOSE TO THE JAIL WHERE PAUL AND SILAS WERE IMPRISONED, THE TREE RINGS WOULD HAVE RECORDED THE EARTHQUAKE THAT DAY.

PAUL'S SECOND JOURNEY WAS WITH HIS FRIEND, SILAS. THEY WENT TO ASIA MINOR, EUROPE AND GREECE.

THE THIRD JOURNEY WAS HIS LONGEST. PAUL WENT TO ASIA MINOR, MACEDONIA AND GREECE.

DID YOU KNOW IN GREECE YOU CAN GO TO JAIL FOR ABANDONING YOUR DOG?

PAUL ONCE TOLD A CRIPPLED MAN TO GET UP AND WALK, ALTHOUGH THE MAN HAD NOT BEEN ABLE TO WALK SINCE BIRTH. AT ONCE THE MAN ROSE TO HIS FEET AND WALKED AS IF HE HAD ALWAYS BEEN ABLE TO.

THE MONTH OF JULY IS NAMED AFTER JULIUS CAESAR. THE MONTH OF AUGUST IS NAMED AFTER AUGUSTUS CAESAR.

HOBBY CORNER

LEARN THE MAPS AS GOOD AS PAUL!

AS YOU KNOW, PAUL WAS A GREAT TRAVELER AS HE TOURED AROUND TO MANY PLACES PREACHING THE WORD OF GOD AND JESUS CHRIST. PAUL MUST HAVE BEEN VERY FAMILIAR WITH MAPS AND YOU CAN BE AS WELL! GET A WORLD MAP FROM YOUR PARENTS AND TACK IT ON THE WALL IN YOUR ROOM. LOCATE PLACES LIKE PARIS, CHINA AND ROME! HAVE YOUR PARENTS ASK YOU WHERE SOMEPLACE IS AND SHOW IT TO THEM. PERHAPS MARK THE PLACES YOU ARE FAMILIAR WITH BY PLACING A TACK ON THEM. WHEN YOU GET GOOD ENOUGH, MAKE A LOG OF THE PLACES YOU WOULD HAVE TO TRAVEL THROUGH IF YOU WENT TO ROME LIKE PAUL DID.

HAPPY TRAVELING!

APPEARANCES OF JESUS AFTER THE RESSURECTION

CHRIST IS A HEBREW WORD MEANING "ANOINTED ONE." TO BE ANOINTED IS TO PUT OIL ON THE BODY AS A SIGN OF SANCTIFICATION OR CONSECRATION.

THE LAST TIME THE DISCIPLES SAW JESUS WAS WHEN HE ASCENDED TO HEAVEN!

DID YOU KNOW THE SUN WAS BIGGER BACK WHEN JESUS WAS RESURRECTED? IN FACT, IN THE LAST HALF CENTURY THE SUN HAS LOST ABOUT 250 MILES OF RADIUS.

JESUS MADE TEN APPEARANCES IN FORTY DAYS TO HIS DISCIPLES.

MARY SAW TWO ANGELS SITTING INSIDE THE TOMB WHERE JESUS WAS LAID TO REST.

MARY MAGDALENE WAS THE FIRST PERSON JESUS APPEARED TO AFTER THE RESURRECTION. HE TOLD MARY SHE COULD NOT TOUCH HIM BECAUSE HE HAD NOT YET ASCENDED TO HEAVEN.

JESUS PROMISED THAT HE WOULD RETURN ONE DAY JUST AS HE HAD GONE.

The seventh Sunday after Easter is called the Pentacost or Whitsunday and it commemorates the descent of the Holy Spirit upon the disciples.

Jesus explained that His reason for returning was to grant the disciples the power of the Holy Spirit and the power to forgive sins.

After Jesus rose from the dead, He appeared to His disciples to comfort and encourage them.

When Jesus appeared to His disciples, Thomas didn't believe it really was Jesus. Jesus asked Thomas to touch the wounds in His hands and the one in His side. Only then did Thomas truly believe. This is where the saying "Doubting Thomas" originated.

HOBBY CORNER

CREATE YOUR OWN ANGEL MOBILES!

What you will need:

A pencil. Yellow and white construction paper, Safety Scissors, Glue, String or yarn

First cut out four pieces of construction paper, all about 8" x 8" square, and make sure that two of the pieces are white and the other two yellow. Fold each square in half. Now, following the diagrams, draw the outlines for the halo, the wings, the angels head and the gown. Cut out the parts and unfold them. You should now have eight shapes for your angel mobile. Lay three of the pieces down flat on the table. The halo should be on top, the head beneath the halo, next the wings and the gown at the bottom. Now take a long piece of string, and starting with one end of the string glue it to the angels gown, then to the wings, next to the head and finally to the halo. Now glue the remaining shapes over the top of the matching shapes; the halo over the other halo shape, etc. Look! You have created your very own angel mobile! Hang it over your bed or someplace where you can look at it and remember the angels in heaven are always watching over you.